SPOT IT

AIRCRAFT

TOP THAT! Kids™

Copyright © 2004 Top That! Publishing plc
Tide Mill Way, Woodbridge, Suffolk, IP12 1AP, UK
www.topthatpublishing.com
Top That! Kids is a Trademark of Top That! Publishing plc

HOW TO USE YOUR SPOT IT GUIDE

Next time you hear a whirring noise in the sky, why not take a closer look? Open your eyes wide to discover all about the planes around you! There's 101 different types to spot.

18

18

Firstly, have fun attaching the specially-shaped stickers onto the outlines on some of the pages. There are matching numbers to help you.

When you've spotted something, stick in one of the round stickers, and make a note of when and where you saw it.

SPOT IT!   GOT IT!

We've also rated the planes according to how likely you are to see them. Ten points means you've spotted and scored an easy target while 60 points means you've found a really rare type! How long will it take you to reach the maximum score of 2,830?

HINTS AND TIPS

- Why not visit an air show or museum? It's a sure-fire way to spot those older planes that are no longer flying.
- Keep your eyes peeled at the airport!
- Remember – whether you see the plane for real, on the Internet, in books, or magazines – they all count as 'Spots'!

EARLY PLANES

PLANE: Sopwith Camel   **CLASS:** WW1 Fighter

DESCRIPTION: This famous aeroplane was the main British fighter of WW1. It duelled with the Fokker Dr.1 (see below) for the title of best fighter of the war. In the end the Camel was the better plane as it was faster and had better visibility.

POINTS VALUE: 40

DATE SPOTTED: SPOT IT!   GOT IT!

WHERE SPOTTED:

PLANE: Fokker Dr.1

CLASS: WW1 Fighter

DESCRIPTION: Best known as the plane flown by Baron Von Richtofen (the Red Baron), this plane's three-winged design gave great manoeuvrability but the extra drag meant that it was much slower than its allied rivals.

POINTS VALUE: 30

DATE SPOTTED: SPOT IT!   GOT IT!

WHERE SPOTTED:

3

PLANE: Royal Aircraft Factory SE5-A

CLASS: Fighter

DESCRIPTION: A strong and sturdy plane with a powerful engine and good visibility, this fighter was flown by many leading British fighter pilots.

POINTS VALUE: 20

DATE SPOTTED: SPOT IT!   GOT IT!

WHERE SPOTTED:

PLANE: DeHavilland Tiger Moth

CLASS: Trainer

DESCRIPTION: This plane is one of the most common early bi-planes still flying in any numbers. You can see them at airshows all over the world. The Tiger Moth was popular with novice pilots as it was so easy to fly. **POINTS VALUE:** 30

DATE SPOTTED: SPOT IT!   GOT IT!

WHERE SPOTTED:

PLANE: Fairy Swordfish

CLASS: Torpedo Bomber

DESCRIPTION: This plane was famous for the torpedo raid that led to the sinking of the German battleship *Bismarck*. Although slow, it was highly regarded by its pilots and nicknamed the 'Stringbag'.

POINTS VALUE: 30

DATE SPOTTED: SPOT IT!   GOT IT!

WHERE SPOTTED:

WARBIRDS

PLANE: Supermarine Spitfire   **CLASS:** WW2 Fighter

DESCRIPTION: One of the most famous planes ever built and perhaps the most beautiful, the Spitfire was decisive in winning the Battle of Britain. The Spitfire entered service in 1938. With eight machine guns, (four in each wing), it had plenty of firepower.

POINTS VALUE: 30

DATE SPOTTED: SPOT IT!   GOT IT!

WHERE SPOTTED:

- -

PLANE: Hawker Hurricane

CLASS: WW2 Fighter

DESCRIPTION: The RAF's first single-winged (monoplane) fighter, the Hurricane was built in greater numbers than the Spitfire and shot down more German aircraft, including German bombers. Only 11 Hurricanes remain flying. **POINTS VALUE:** 40

DATE SPOTTED: SPOT IT!   GOT IT!

WHERE SPOTTED:

PLANE: Focke Wulf FW190 **CLASS:** WW2 Fighter

DESCRIPTION: The FW190 was the best German fighter of the war. It was designed to out-fly and out-fight the Spitfire. The FW190 was used in many different roles such as fighter, light bomber and ground attack plane, and dominated the skies after its introduction in August 1941. **POINTS VALUE:** 50

DATE SPOTTED: | **SPOT IT!** | **GOT IT!**

WHERE SPOTTED:

- -

PLANE: Northrop Grumman Bearcat

CLASS: WW2 Fighter

DESCRIPTION: The Bearcat was the last American fighter of the war, entering service only a few months before the end of the fighting. The Bearcat combined a hugely powerful engine with a light body to give maximum performance. **POINTS VALUE:** 30

DATE SPOTTED: | **SPOT IT!** | **GOT IT!**

WHERE SPOTTED:

PLANE: Avro Lancaster   **CLASS:** WW2 bomber

DESCRIPTION: The Lancaster
was the biggest RAF
bomber of WW2.
Used as a night
bomber,
the Lancaster
also carried
the famous
Bouncing Bombs used in
the Dambusters raid. It had
four engines and was heavily
protected by machine guns found in
rotating turrets in the nose, tail, belly and top.
POINTS VALUE: 50

DATE SPOTTED: **SPOT IT!**   **GOT IT!**

WHERE SPOTTED:

PLANE: Boeing B-29 Superfortress

CLASS: WW2 Bomber

DESCRIPTION: The last US
bomber of WW2, the
Superfortress flew higher
than any other aircraft
of the war and had
an impressive range
of 5,955 km
(3,700 miles). In
1945 the B-29 *Enola
Gay* dropped the first
ever atomic bomb on
Hiroshima. **POINTS VALUE:** 30

DATE SPOTTED: **SPOT IT!**   **GOT IT!**

WHERE SPOTTED:

PLANE: Messerschmitt Me109

CLASS: WW2 Fighter

DESCRIPTION: The most often-used German fighter of WW2, the Me109 was fast, manoeuvrable and heavily armed. The 109's main weakness was that take off and landing was always quite tricky.

POINTS VALUE: 30

DATE SPOTTED: **SPOT IT!**   **GOT IT!**

WHERE SPOTTED:

- -

PLANE: P-51 Mustang

CLASS: WW2 Fighter

DESCRIPTION: This was the famous US fighter of WW2. The P-51 was the best fighter of the war. Heavily armed, fast and very strong, American pilots loved their P-51s, giving many of them ladylike names such as *Glamorous Glennis* and *Mary Jane*. **POINTS VALUE:** 20

3

DATE SPOTTED: **SPOT IT!**   **GOT IT!**

WHERE SPOTTED:

PLANE: P-47 Thunderbolt　**CLASS:** WW2 Fighter

DESCRIPTION: This US fighter was big and heavy. Its pilots loved it because it was so tough it was almost impossible to shoot down. The Thunderbolt was an escort fighter, protecting the squadrons of Flying Fortresses. **POINTS VALUE:** 30

DATE SPOTTED:　**SPOT IT!**　**GOT IT!**

WHERE SPOTTED:

- -

PLANE: B-17 Flying Fortress

CLASS: WW2 Bomber

DESCRIPTION: Called the Flying Fortress because of the number of guns it carried, this four-engined heavy bomber flew daylight bombing raids over Germany during WW2. **POINTS VALUE:** 20

DATE SPOTTED:　**SPOT IT!**　**GOT IT!**

WHERE SPOTTED:

- -

PLANE: Mitsubishi Zero　**CLASS:** WW2 Fighter

DESCRIPTION: The Zero was the best Japanese fighter of WW2. It was fast, very light and could compete with giants like the Hawker Hurricane and P40B Tomahawk American fighter that flew against it. The Japanese pilots were also very well trained. **POINTS VALUE:** 40

DATE SPOTTED:　**SPOT IT!**　**GOT IT!**

WHERE SPOTTED:

PLANE: Lockheed P-38 Lightning

CLASS: WW2 Fighter

DESCRIPTION: This fighter is famous for its distinctive twin tail booms. With two powerful engines it was fast and agile. The Germans called it the 'fork tailed devil', and it was certainly dangerous with its four nose mounted cannon. Only seven remain flying – you'd be lucky to spot this one in the air! **POINTS VALUE:** 50

DATE SPOTTED: **SPOT IT!**   **GOT IT!**

WHERE SPOTTED:

PLANE: DeHavilland Mosquito

CLASS: WW2 Fighter Bomber

DESCRIPTION: Known as the Wooden Wonder, the Mosquito was one of the fastest planes of the war. It was an effective fighter and light bomber but was most useful guiding Allied bombers over Europe on pathfinder missions as well as aerial photography. **POINTS VALUE:** 40

DATE SPOTTED: **SPOT IT!**   **GOT IT!**

WHERE SPOTTED:

PLANE: Douglas Dakota   **CLASS:** Transport

DESCRIPTION: Correctly known as the DC3, this is one of the world's most recognised planes. Introduced during WW2 as a transport plane, Dakotas are still flying all over the world doing all kinds of jobs from fire fighting to the provision of inexpensive commercial flights. **POINTS VALUE:** 10

DATE SPOTTED: **SPOT IT!**   **GOT IT!**

WHERE SPOTTED:

PLANE: Grumman Hellcat   **CLASS:** WW2 Fighter

DESCRIPTION: This was the main US carrier-based fighter of WW2 and entered service with the US Navy in 1942. It was clearly superior to any Japanese fighter with a top speed of 605 kph (376 mph) and six wing-mounted machine guns. **POINTS VALUE:** 40

4

DATE SPOTTED: **SPOT IT!**   **GOT IT!**

WHERE SPOTTED:

HISTORIC JETS

PLANE: F-86 Sabre   **CLASS:** Jet Fighter

DESCRIPTION: One of the first jet fighters, the Sabre fought during the Korean war against the very similar MiG-15. The Sabre could fly supersonic (faster than the speed of sound) in a shallow dive and was flown by airforces all over the world. **POINTS VALUE:** 20

DATE SPOTTED: **SPOT IT!**   **GOT IT!**

WHERE SPOTTED:

PLANE: Mig 15   **CLASS:** Jet Fighter

DESCRIPTION: The first Soviet jet fighter (known as the 'aircraft soldier') flew against the Sabre in the Korean war. Although the MiG was the better aircraft, the more aggressive US pilots shot down many Russian MiGs. **POINTS VALUE:** 40

DATE SPOTTED: **SPOT IT!**   **GOT IT!**

WHERE SPOTTED:

(**PLANE:** Gloucester Meteor)

(**CLASS:** WW2 Fighter)

DESCRIPTION: The first operational
Allied jet fighter entered service
with the RAF in 1945. There were
too few to make much difference in
air combat but its speed proved very useful
in shooting down V1 flying bombs. **POINTS VALUE:** 40

(**DATE SPOTTED:**) (**SPOT IT!**) (**GOT IT!**)

(**WHERE SPOTTED:**)

- -

(**PLANE:** F-100 Super Sabre)

(**CLASS:** Jet Fighter)

DESCRIPTION: The Super Sabre
was the first jet fighter able to
go supersonic in level flight. It
entered service in 1954 and in its
final specification it could reach over
1,368 kph (850 mph) Mach 1.3. **POINTS VALUE:** 30

(**DATE SPOTTED:**) (**SPOT IT!**) (**GOT IT!**)

(**WHERE SPOTTED:**)

- -

(**PLANE:** Messerschmitt Me262) (**CLASS:** WW2 Fighter)

DESCRIPTION: The Me262 was the first
operational jet fighter of WW2.
Despite its greater speed, too few
Me262s were built and many
were wasted as bombers. The Me262
is now a very rare aircraft but modern
replicas can be built and flown, some having two
seats, others with one. **POINTS VALUE:** 60

(**DATE SPOTTED:**) (**SPOT IT!**) (**GOT IT!**)

(**WHERE SPOTTED:**)

13

PLANE: McDonald Douglas Phantom

CLASS: Jet Fighter

DESCRIPTION: The Phantom was a superb multi-role fighter flying from land and sea and for many airforces around the world, where it was used as a fighter, bomber and interceptor. It was the first fighter to have no cannon, using missiles to shoot down its targets. **POINTS VALUE:** 10

6

DATE SPOTTED: **SPOT IT!**   **GOT IT!**

WHERE SPOTTED:

PLANE: English Electric Lightning

CLASS: Jet Fighter

DESCRIPTION: The most advanced fighter of its day, the Lightning was fast even by modern standards. It was particularly famous for its ability to go supersonic in a steep climb, as it was designed to intercept high-flying Russian bombers. **POINTS VALUE:** 60

DATE SPOTTED: **SPOT IT!**   **GOT IT!**

WHERE SPOTTED:

PLANE: Avro Vulcan **CLASS:** Jet Bomber

DESCRIPTION: This giant aircraft was the RAF's first nuclear bomber, designed to reach deep into Russia and drop its bombs. The Vulcan entered service in 1956 and was still flying in 1982. Look out for its distinctive delta wing. **POINTS VALUE:** 50

DATE SPOTTED: **SPOT IT!** **GOT IT!**

WHERE SPOTTED:

• •

PLANE: Hawker Hunter **CLASS:** Jet Fighter

DESCRIPTION: A classic early jet fighter, the Hunter entered service with the RAF in 1954. There are still many Hunters still flying and they are popular visitors to air shows all over the world. **POINTS VALUE:** 20

DATE SPOTTED: **SPOT IT!** **GOT IT!**

WHERE SPOTTED:

• •

PLANE: Lockheed Starfighter **CLASS:** Jet Fighter

DESCRIPTION: This graceful fighter could fly at up to Mach 2.2–2,334 kph (1,450 mph) and saw service with many air forces. The German air force flew many Starfighters but had so many accidents that it became known as 'the widowmaker'. **POINTS VALUE:** 20

DATE SPOTTED: **SPOT IT!** **GOT IT!**

WHERE SPOTTED:

COMMERCIAL AIRLINERS

PLANE: Airbus A300 **CLASS:** Airliner

DESCRIPTION: The A300 was very advanced when it was introduced, with its computerised flight deck. This twin-engined plane can carry 266 passengers in first and second class. It is the world's most popular mid-sized airliner. **POINTS VALUE:** 10

DATE SPOTTED: **SPOT IT!** **GOT IT!**

WHERE SPOTTED:

PLANE: Airbus A320 **CLASS:** Airliner

DESCRIPTION: This small twin-engined airliner is known as a 'single isle' as it only has one aisle of seats. The A320 has a sister aircraft, the A318, which looks the same. With only one aisle there is only room for 122 passengers on board. **POINTS VALUE:** 10

DATE SPOTTED: **SPOT IT!** **GOT IT!**

WHERE SPOTTED:

PLANE: Boeing 747 **CLASS:** Airliner

DESCRIPTION: The first 747 flew one month before the first Concorde in 1969. Since then it has gone on to become the most successful civil airliner of all. **POINTS VALUE:** 10

DATE SPOTTED: **SPOT IT!** **GOT IT!**

WHERE SPOTTED:

- -

PLANE: Boeing 767

CLASS: Airliner

DESCRIPTION: The 767 is actually a whole family of twin-engined aircraft. The first of the family flew in 1981, the latest was introduced in 1999. The 767 is able to fly non stop from London to Tokyo. It flies across the Atlantic more often than all other jetliners joined together. **POINTS VALUE:** 20

DATE SPOTTED: **SPOT IT!** **GOT IT!**

WHERE SPOTTED:

- -

PLANE: Boeing 737 **CLASS:** Airliner

DESCRIPTION: Over 5,300 of these popular aircraft are currently flying around the world. The latest version uses 'winglets', turned up ends to the wings, to increase its fuel efficiency and carrying capacity. **POINTS VALUE:** 10

DATE SPOTTED: **SPOT IT!** **GOT IT!**

WHERE SPOTTED:

PLANE: SAAB 340 **CLASS:** Airliner

DESCRIPTION: Made jointly with the US aircraft company Fairchild, this plane is built for short hops. It carries 37 passengers. Shorter flights mean that it is more economic to use turbo-prop engines. The 340 has two engines that develop 1,730 horsepower.

POINTS VALUE: 30

DATE SPOTTED: **SPOT IT!** **GOT IT!**

WHERE SPOTTED:

PLANE: Douglas DC-10 **CLASS:** Airliner

DESCRIPTION: The DC-10 has been in service for over 30 years and is flown all over the world. It is a particular favourite with cargo and delivery companies such as Federal Express and DHL. **POINTS VALUE:** 10

DATE SPOTTED: **SPOT IT!** **GOT IT!**

WHERE SPOTTED:

PLANE: Boeing 727   **CLASS:** Airliner

DESCRIPTION: The 727 was the first ever tri-jet, that is a jet with two wing and one tail engine. This makes it easy to spot among other aircraft.

8

POINTS VALUE: 10

DATE SPOTTED: **SPOT IT!**   **GOT IT!**

WHERE SPOTTED:

• •

PLANE: BAE 146

CLASS: Airliner

DESCRIPTION: The BAE 146 was designed for short city-to-city journeys. Because it often takes off from and lands in city airports it only needs very short runways, and is one of the quietest aircraft in the air. **POINTS VALUE:** 20

DATE SPOTTED: **SPOT IT!**   **GOT IT!**

WHERE SPOTTED:

• •

PLANE: Fokker Friendship   **CLASS:** Airliner

DESCRIPTION: The Friendship first entered service in 1955. It was intended to replace the Douglas Dakota. It is a tough, reliable aircraft, well suited to more difficult and remote operations away from major city routes. **POINTS VALUE:** 30

DATE SPOTTED: **SPOT IT!**   **GOT IT!**

WHERE SPOTTED:

PLANE: BAE Concorde **CLASS:** Airliner

DESCRIPTION: The world's only supersonic airliner first flew in 1969 and carried passengers at over twice the speed of sound until the end of 2003. Probably the most beautiful aircraft ever built, it had many unique features such as a famous drooping nose, and distinctive delta wings.

POINTS VALUE: 20

DATE SPOTTED: | **SPOT IT!** | **GOT IT!**

WHERE SPOTTED:

PLANE: Airbus A300ST **CLASS:** Transport

DESCRIPTION: This bizarre machine is designed to transport large aircraft parts, such as wing assemblies and fuselages, between Airbus factories in the UK and France. It is also known as the Beluga, after the whale. **POINTS VALUE:** 40

9

DATE SPOTTED: | **SPOT IT!** | **GOT IT!**

WHERE SPOTTED:

PLANE: DeHavilland DHC-8   **CLASS:** Airliner

DESCRIPTION: Known as the 'Dash 8' this aircraft was designed and built by DeHavilland in Canada. When DeHavilland were bought by Bombardier Aircraft the plane was re-named the Bombardier Q100 (Q for quiet). They are known for their reliability. **POINTS VALUE:** 30

DATE SPOTTED: **SPOT IT!**   **GOT IT!**

WHERE SPOTTED:

PLANE: Boeing 777   **CLASS:** Airliner

DESCRIPTION: The newest member of the Boeing family, the 777 is the first airliner to be designed entirely on a computer. The whole aircraft was modelled piece by piece in 3-D so that no prototypes were needed. **POINTS VALUE:** 20

DATE SPOTTED: **SPOT IT!**   **GOT IT!**

WHERE SPOTTED:

PLANE: Boeing 707   **CLASS:** Airliner

DESCRIPTION: The 707 was the first modern jet-liner, entering service in 1958. Despite its age it is still used by many smaller airlines, particularly in far-flung parts of the world. The 707 forms the basis for the USAF's KC-135 tanker. It has a wingspan of 39 m (130 feet).

POINTS VALUE: 30

DATE SPOTTED: **SPOT IT!**   **GOT IT!**

WHERE SPOTTED:

PLANE: Douglas DC-9

CLASS: Airliner

DESCRIPTION: The DC-9 was first manufactured in 1965 and it remains in production today. This long life makes it a very common spot at airports all over the world. Its distinctive long tin shape helps it stand out from more modern airliners.

POINTS VALUE: 10

DATE SPOTTED: **SPOT IT!**   **GOT IT!**

WHERE SPOTTED:

PLANE: Lockheed Tristar   **CLASS:** Airliner

DESCRIPTION: The TriStar is a medium-sized wide bodied jet. It entered service in 1972 and has been flying ever since. Its three-engined design allows the Tristar to fly long distances on the minimum of fuel, making it an efficient and popular aircraft. **POINTS VALUE:** 20

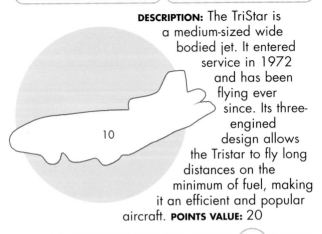

10

DATE SPOTTED: **SPOT IT!**   **GOT IT!**

WHERE SPOTTED:

- -

PLANE: Antanov An-124

CLASS: Transport

DESCRIPTION:
The An-124 is the world's largest aircraft. The hole at the end of the plane lifts open to allow enormous loads of up to 120 tons to be carried. The landing gear of this plane retracts allowing the plane to 'kneel down' for easier loading. **POINTS VALUE:** 40

DATE SPOTTED: **SPOT IT!**   **GOT IT!**

WHERE SPOTTED:

LIGHT AIRCRAFT

PLANE: Beechcraft Bonanza

CLASS: Light Aircraft

DESCRIPTION: This small single-piston-engined plane is very popular with both commercial pilots and individual owners. It can carry five people (pilot plus four passengers) and has a range of just over 1,000 miles. It can reach over 321 kph (200 mph). **POINTS VALUE:** 20

DATE SPOTTED: **SPOT IT!**   **GOT IT!**

WHERE SPOTTED:

PLANE: Beechcraft Baron   **CLASS:** Light Aircraft

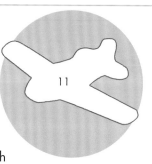

DESCRIPTION: This aircraft is a small twin-piston-engined plane. Often seen around small local airfields, you can sometimes spot it taxiing between the jets at bigger airports. It can fly at up to 370 kph (230 mph) with five passengers. **POINTS VALUE:** 20

DATE SPOTTED: **SPOT IT!**   **GOT IT!**

WHERE SPOTTED:

PLANE: Piper Warrior III   **CLASS:** Light Aircraft

DESCRIPTION: This small plane is designed to be the choice of a beginner pilot. It is built to be easy to fly and simple to maintain. Its 160 hp single piston engine can pull the plane at up to 354 kph (220 mph)!

POINTS VALUE: 10

DATE SPOTTED:	SPOT IT!	GOT IT!
WHERE SPOTTED:		

- -

PLANE: Piper Seneca V

CLASS: Light Aircraft

DESCRIPTION: The Seneca V is the latest version of the best selling twin-engined light aircraft. Its two Teledyne engines are turbo-charged for extra power, and its sleek shape is designed for maximum speed. **POINTS VALUE:** 20

DATE SPOTTED:	SPOT IT!	GOT IT!
WHERE SPOTTED:		

- -

PLANE: BAE Systems Jetstream 32

CLASS: Light Aircraft

DESCRIPTION: This small, twin-engined plane is often seen as a corporate plane used by businessmen to fly to meetings, although many can also be seen at small regional airports all over the world. They have seats for nineteen passengers. **POINTS VALUE:** 20

DATE SPOTTED:	SPOT IT!	GOT IT!
WHERE SPOTTED:		

(**PLANE:** Beech KingAir 350) (**CLASS:** Light aircraft)

DESCRIPTION: The KingAir 350 is designed for use as a corporate plane or for small charter companies. It can carry between nine and fifteen passengers in comfort and with speed. With its two powerful piston engines it can reach 514 kph (320 mph). **POINTS VALUE:** 20

| DATE SPOTTED: | SPOT IT! | GOT IT! |
| WHERE SPOTTED: | | |

(**PLANE:** Piper Chipmunk) (**CLASS:** Light aircraft)

12

DESCRIPTION: This small plane is popular all over the world with private pilots as it is an ideal personal plane. Its manoeuvrability and low weight also make it capable of performing reasonable acrobatics although it is no match for dedicated stunt planes. **POINTS VALUE:** 10

| DATE SPOTTED: | SPOT IT! | GOT IT! |
| WHERE SPOTTED: | | |

PLANE: Gulfstream V

CLASS: Light aircraft

DESCRIPTION: The V is the state of the art in light business jets. It currently holds four city-to-city speed records set in one marathon round the world flight in 2003. It is powered by two Rolls-Royce high efficiency turbo fan engines.

POINTS VALUE: 30

DATE SPOTTED:

WHERE SPOTTED:

SPOT IT!

GOT IT!

• •

PLANE: Piper Cub

CLASS: Light aircraft

DESCRIPTION: Piper manufactured 20,000 'cubs' between 1938 and 1947. It was so popular that the term 'Cub' became used to describe any aircraft of this type. Several companies now make replicas of this small plane so it is quite easy to spot.

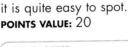

POINTS VALUE: 20

DATE SPOTTED:

WHERE SPOTTED:

SPOT IT!

GOT IT!

27

MILITARY AIRCRAFT

PLANE: Lockheed Hercules C130J

CLASS: Military Transport

DESCRIPTION: In service all over the world, the Hercules is the workhorse of the skies. It is built to carry any military equipment or stores into and out of airfields anywhere in the world. It can take off or land in a very short space.

POINTS VALUE: 20

DATE SPOTTED: | **SPOT IT!** | **GOT IT!**

WHERE SPOTTED:

PLANE: Lockheed Galaxy | **CLASS:** Military Transport

DESCRIPTION: This monster aircraft is the second-largest plane flying today. It loads its cargo through its nose which opens up like a giant mouth. It can carry over 375 tons of cargo and land on very rough surfaces.

POINTS VALUE: 30

DATE SPOTTED: | **SPOT IT!** | **GOT IT!**

WHERE SPOTTED:

PLANE: Northrop Grumman F14 Tomcat

CLASS: Navy Fighter

DESCRIPTION: The Tomcat is the US Navy's premier carrier-based fighter. Its swept wings change shape. When flying at great heights and at top speeds, the wings are swept back. They extend forwards on slow landing. **POINTS VALUE:** 20

DATE SPOTTED: **SPOT IT!**   **GOT IT!**

WHERE SPOTTED:

· ·

PLANE: Northrop Grumman Prowler

CLASS: Electronic Surveillance

DESCRIPTION: The Prowler is packed full of electronics and radar equipment. It spies out possible dangers and then helps to track them down for the other aircraft to destroy. **POINTS VALUE:** 30

DATE SPOTTED: **SPOT IT!**   **GOT IT!**

WHERE SPOTTED:

· ·

PLANE: Boeing E3 Sentry   **CLASS:** AWACS

DESCRIPTION: Easily spotted by the giant, slowly-turning rotodome on top of its fuselage, the Sentry is designed to take control of any battle field. Its computers sort out where all the units are and direct forces to intercept and attack. **POINTS VALUE:** 30

DATE SPOTTED: **SPOT IT!**   **GOT IT!**

WHERE SPOTTED:

PLANE: E6 J-Star   **CLASS:** Communications

DESCRIPTION: This plain looking aircraft is packed full of high-tech equipment and computers. Its role is to allow communications between all forces during a battle. It allows generals to fight wars from many miles away.

POINTS VALUE: 40

DATE SPOTTED: **SPOT IT!**   **GOT IT!**

WHERE SPOTTED:

PLANE: Boeing B-1B Lancer   **CLASS:** Heavy Bomber

DESCRIPTION: The B1B is a supersonic bomber. It has variable geometry (swing) wings like a fighter to allow it a high top speed as well as the ability to carry heavy loads at take off. It can carry nuclear as well as conventional weapons. **POINTS VALUE:** 40

DATE SPOTTED: **SPOT IT!**   **GOT IT!**

WHERE SPOTTED:

PLANE: BOEING B-2 Spirit   CLASS: Heavy Bomber

DESCRIPTION: The B-2's weird shape is designed to make it invisible to enemy radar and missiles. Although it looks pretty space-aged the shape is actually a development of flying wing experiments from the 1950s. It uses 'low observable' technology to penetrate enemy defences. **POINTS VALUE:** 50

DATE SPOTTED: SPOT IT!   GOT IT!

WHERE SPOTTED:

. . . .

PLANE: Lockheed Martin F-117A Nighthawk

CLASS: Fighter Bomber

DESCRIPTION: Although it is known as the stealth fighter, the F-117 is actually more of a bomber. The strange flat surfaces deflect radar and its engines are shielded to reduce heat emissions, so it can attack undetected. **POINTS VALUE:** 40

14

DATE SPOTTED: SPOT IT!   GOT IT!

WHERE SPOTTED:

PLANE: F15 Eagle   **CLASS:** Fighter

DESCRIPTION: The F-15 Eagle is probably the world's best fighter aircraft. First built in 1975, constant upgrades have kept it ahead of all other fighters. With a top speed of 3,018 kph (1,875 mph) it can fly at two and a half times the speed of sound.

POINTS VALUE: 30

DATE SPOTTED: **SPOT IT!**   **GOT IT!**

WHERE SPOTTED:

- -

PLANE: Boeing F/A-18 Hornet   **CLASS:** Fighter

DESCRIPTION: The F/A-18 is the US Navy's primary strike fighter. While the F-14 protects the fleet, the Hornet is designed to attack and destroy enemy ground or air targets in all weather conditions and by day or night.

POINTS VALUE: 30

DATE SPOTTED: **SPOT IT!**   **GOT IT!**

WHERE SPOTTED:

PLANE: Fairchild Republic A-10 Thunderbolt

CLASS: Ground Attack

DESCRIPTION: No other plane looks like the A-10! It is designed to attack enemy units on the ground using missiles and its giant 'Avenger' nose-mounted cannon, the biggest aircraft gun in the world. **POINTS VALUE:** 20

DATE SPOTTED: | **SPOT IT!** | **GOT IT!**

WHERE SPOTTED:

· ·

PLANE: Panavia Tornado

CLASS: Multi-role

15

DESCRIPTION: The Tornado is a very flexible, heavily armed aircraft. As good a fighter as a bomber it is also used in reconnaissance (information finding missions because of its high top speed of 2,334 kph (1,450 mph). **POINTS VALUE:** 20

DATE SPOTTED: | **SPOT IT!** | **GOT IT!**

WHERE SPOTTED:

· ·

PLANE: SEPECAT Jaguar

CLASS: Interceptor

DESCRIPTION: The Jaguar is flown by many airforces around the world. You can spot it quite easily because many are equipped with distinctive missile pylons on top of their wings instead of under. **POINTS VALUE:** 30

DATE SPOTTED: | **SPOT IT!** | **GOT IT!**

WHERE SPOTTED:

PLANE: F-22 Raptor

CLASS: Fighter

DESCRIPTION: The Raptor is the USAF's brand new fighter. It is a semi-stealth design that uses the latest computers to allow it to out-fly and out-fight any enemy aircraft that is likely to be built for the foreseeable future.

POINTS VALUE: 30

DATE SPOTTED:

SPOT IT!

GOT IT!

WHERE SPOTTED:

PLANE: Lockheed SR-71 Blackbird

CLASS: Spy Plane

DESCRIPTION: This famous spy plane is able to fly to the edge of space and at nearly three times the speed of sound. It was too fast and flew too high to be shot down by any aircraft or missile. An SR-71 holds the all time trans-atlantic speed record. **POINTS VALUE:** 60

16

DATE SPOTTED:

SPOT IT!

GOT IT!

WHERE SPOTTED:

PLANE: AV-8 Harrier **CLASS:** Fighter

DESCRIPTION: The Harrier is famously the only operational plane in the world that can take off and land vertically, (VTOL). This ability makes the Harrier an extremely agile fighter although it is also slow by modern standards. **POINTS VALUE:** 20

DATE SPOTTED: **SPOT IT!**   **GOT IT!**

WHERE SPOTTED:

· ·

PLANE: T-38 Talon **CLASS:** Military Trainer

DESCRIPTION: This small jet trainer is used by the USAF to introduce pilots to flying fast jets. It has two powerful engines and can fly supersonic to give pilots an accurate taste of what front line combat aircraft can do. **POINTS VALUE:** 30

DATE SPOTTED: **SPOT IT!**   **GOT IT!**

WHERE SPOTTED:

· ·

PLANE: Lockheed Martin P-3 Orion

CLASS: Sub-Hunter

DESCRIPTION: The Orion is used by many navies to find and destroy enemy submarines. It searches for subs using sonar and Magnetic Anomaly Detectors. When it finds one, it uses its armament of torpedoes to close in for the kill. **POINTS VALUE:** 30

DATE SPOTTED: **SPOT IT!**   **GOT IT!**

WHERE SPOTTED:

PLANE: BAE Systems Hawk

CLASS: Trainer

DESCRIPTION: The Hawk is the world's most popular jet trainer. They are used to introduce pilots to jet flight. The Hawk is also famous as the plane used by the RAF's famous acrobatic team, The Red Arrows, which perform amazing stunts. **POINTS VALUE:** 20

DATE SPOTTED: **SPOT IT!**   **GOT IT!**

WHERE SPOTTED:

PLANE: Lockheed JSF   **CLASS:** Multi-role fighter

DESCRIPTION: The JSF is the future of military aviation. Built jointly by the US and UK, the plane provides cutting-edge stealth technology for the airforce and navy of both countries. It will also be used by the US marine corps. The JSF is so complicated only its computers can keep it flying. **POINTS VALUE:** 60

DATE SPOTTED: **SPOT IT!**   **GOT IT!**

WHERE SPOTTED:

PLANE: Boeing B52   **CLASS:** Heavy Bomber

DESCRIPTION: This heavy bomber entered service with the USAF in the sixties and is planned to still be in use until 2050, making it one of the longest lived weapons of any kind. It carries a huge bomb load and has seen action in every US conflict from Vietnam to the Gulf. It is also known by its pilots as the BUF (Big Ugly Fellow). **POINTS VALUE:** 20

DATE SPOTTED: **SPOT IT!**   **GOT IT!**

WHERE SPOTTED:

- -

PLANE: Eurofighter Typhoon

CLASS: Multi-role fighter

DESCRIPTION: The Typhoon is Europe's key fighter for the next 50 years. Just entering service it is often seen displaying its fantastic speed and agility at air shows. The Typhoon will be flown by most European air forces except the French. **POINTS VALUE:** 30

17

DATE SPOTTED: **SPOT IT!**   **GOT IT!**

WHERE SPOTTED:

PLANE: SAAB Gripen **CLASS:** Fighter

DESCRIPTION: In service with the Swedish and South African air force as well as many others, the Gripen is quite a simple plane by modern standards. A third of the frame is made from composites which are very light yet strong. It is a relatively cheap plane to build and maintain, yet it can fly at twice the speed of sound. **POINTS VALUE:** 20

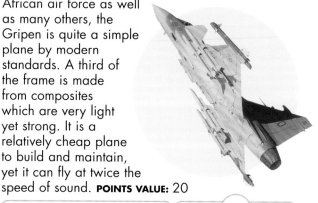

DATE SPOTTED: **SPOT IT!**   **GOT IT!**

WHERE SPOTTED:

PLANE: Lockheed U2 (TSR) **CLASS:** Spy Plane

DESCRIPTION: Created during the Cold War to spy on Russia, the U2 is still used to gather intelligence all over the world. Although the Russians could detect the plane on radar, it flew at such heights that it was out of their missile range and they couldn't shoot it down. It is also used by NASA as a research plane to gather information on space.

POINTS VALUE: 60

DATE SPOTTED: **SPOT IT!**   **GOT IT!**

WHERE SPOTTED:

PLANE: BAE Systems Nimrod

CLASS: Reconnaissance

DESCRIPTION: Developed from the Comet airliner in the sixties, the Nimrod is the RAF's main maritime patrol craft. Its long range allows it to fly great distances over water in search and rescue missions. **POINTS VALUE:** 20

DATE SPOTTED: | **SPOT IT!** | **GOT IT!**

WHERE SPOTTED:

PLANE: T-6A Texan

CLASS: Military Trainer

18

DESCRIPTION: The T-6A is the plane that most beginner pilots of the American Air Force Learn to fly. The latest version is called the Texan. It is fully aerobatic to allow pilots to learn difficult manoeuvres. In civilian guise it is called the Beech PC-9. **POINTS VALUE:** 30

DATE SPOTTED: | **SPOT IT!** | **GOT IT!**

WHERE SPOTTED:

PLANE: KC-135 | **CLASS:** Tanker

DESCRIPTION: The KC-135 is a giant flying petrol station! It allows other planes to refuel in mid-air in order to give them greater range. The fuel is dispensed from a boom (a large pipe-like attachment) at the rear of the plane. **POINTS VALUE:** 20

DATE SPOTTED: | **SPOT IT!** | **GOT IT!**

WHERE SPOTTED:

PLANE: F-16 Fighting Falcon

CLASS: Fighter

DESCRIPTION: The F-16 is an ultra lightweight, high-performance fighter. It can fly at up to 2,414 kph (1,500 mph) and has a good range. Because of its simplicity and reliability the F-16 Falcon is the most numerous fighter aircraft in the west.

POINTS VALUE: 20

DATE SPOTTED: **SPOT IT!**   **GOT IT!**

WHERE SPOTTED:

PLANE: General Dynamics F-111

CLASS: Fighter Bomber

DESCRIPTION: Often called the Aardvark because of the shape of its nose, the F-111 fulfilled many roles in the US air force from tactical bomber to 'wild weasel' missions. The crew are protected by a unique cockpit escape capsule. **POINTS VALUE:** 30

19

DATE SPOTTED: **SPOT IT!**   **GOT IT!**

WHERE SPOTTED:

PLANE: Northrop Grumman E-2 Hawkeye

CLASS: AWACS

DESCRIPTION: Since 1964, the Hawkeye has been in service as the US Navy's electronic information gatherer. The rotodome (circular rotating dome) on the fuselage scans the sky and sea for enemy aircraft and directs attack fighters to their targets. **POINTS VALUE:** 40

DATE SPOTTED: | **SPOT IT!** | **GOT IT!**

WHERE SPOTTED:

- -

PLANE: Boeing C-17 Globemaster

CLASS: Heavy Transport

DESCRIPTION: Designed to take off and land from short and damaged runways (VSTOL), the Globemaster can load nearly 75 tons through its opening tail ramp. It has a crew of three, two pilots and a loadmaster. **POINTS VALUE:** 20

DATE SPOTTED: | **SPOT IT!** | **GOT IT!**

WHERE SPOTTED:

HELICOPTERS

PLANE: GKN Westland Lynx

CLASS: Military Helicopter

DESCRIPTION: This helicopter is commonly used by all branches of the British military. It is one of the fastest helicopters in the world and is one of the only models to be able to fly inverted (upside down) or to perform a complete loop. **POINTS VALUE:** 20

DATE SPOTTED: **SPOT IT!**   **GOT IT!**

WHERE SPOTTED:

PLANE: Boeing Sea Knight

CLASS: Military Transport

DESCRIPTION: The Sea Knight is the US Marine Corps main transport helicopter. It has two sets of rotors, one at the front, the other at the rear to provide the lifting power to carry heavy military equipment and troops into battle.
POINTS VALUE: 30

DATE SPOTTED: **SPOT IT!**   **GOT IT!**

WHERE SPOTTED:

PLANE: Westland Sea King

CLASS: SAR helicopter

DESCRIPTION: The Sea King is used by navies and airforces in many countries as a SAR (Search and Rescue) helicopter. If you are stranded at sea it is most likely that you will be winched to safety by a Sea King!

POINTS VALUE: 10

20

DATE SPOTTED: SPOT IT!   GOT IT!

WHERE SPOTTED:

· ·

PLANE: Aerospatial Puma

CLASS: Medium Transport

DESCRIPTION: Nearly 700 Pumas are flying around the world with both military and civilian owners. Civilian versions are known as Cougars, and are sometimes used for VIP transport. Powered by two powerful turbo shaft engines, the Puma can carry up to 5 tons of cargo. POINTS VALUE: 30

DATE SPOTTED: SPOT IT!   GOT IT!

WHERE SPOTTED:

PLANE: Boeing AH-64D Apache Longbow

CLASS: Attack Helicopter

DESCRIPTION: This fearsome helicopter is bristling with missiles and machine guns. It is heavily armoured to allow it to survive over the battlefield as it hunts down and destroys enemy tanks with its nose mounted machine gun or Hellfire rockets. **POINTS VALUE:** 40

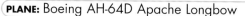

DATE SPOTTED: **SPOT IT!** **GOT IT!**

WHERE SPOTTED:

PLANE: Bell UH-1   **CLASS:** Utility Helicopter

DESCRIPTION: This is probably the worlds most recognisable helicopter. The UH-1 is better known as the Huey and is famous for its role as a troop carrier and gunship during the Vietnam war. It is also popular with civilian pilots. **POINTS VALUE:** 10

DATE SPOTTED: **SPOT IT!** **GOT IT!**

WHERE SPOTTED:

PLANE: Bell Huey Cobra **CLASS:** Gunship

DESCRIPTION: Developed from the UH-1 as a dedicated gunship, the Cobra was introduced during the Vietnam war. Its two pilots sit one in front of the other to give the helicopter the narrowest, and most versatile shape possible. **POINTS VALUE:** 40

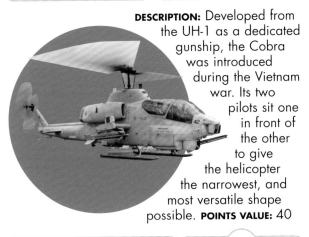

DATE SPOTTED: | **SPOT IT!** | **GOT IT!**

WHERE SPOTTED:

....

PLANE: Robinson R22 **CLASS:** Light Helicopter

DESCRIPTION: The R22 is a budget helicopter. It is powered by a piston engine rather than the expensive turbine engines of larger machines. This makes it very popular with owner/flyers and helicopter schools, where people gain their licences.
POINTS VALUE: 10

21

DATE SPOTTED: | **SPOT IT!** | **GOT IT!**

WHERE SPOTTED:

PLANE: Bell Jet Ranger **CLASS:** Business

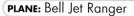

DESCRIPTION: The Jet Ranger is the most popular business helicopter in the world. Its simple design and reliability mean that you can see them at airports everywhere. There is also a military version for training pilots.

POINTS VALUE: 10

DATE SPOTTED: **SPOT IT!** **GOT IT!**

WHERE SPOTTED:

PLANE: Boeing Chinook

CLASS: Heavy Transport

DESCRIPTION: The Chinook is often seen on the TV News, lifting troops and heavy equipment in and out of combat. With its two powerful engines it can carry nearly 28 tons of cargo, so one Chinook can take the place of three smaller helicopters. **POINTS VALUE:** 20

DATE SPOTTED: **SPOT IT!** **GOT IT!**

WHERE SPOTTED:

(**PLANE:** Eurocopter Squirrel)

(**CLASS:** Light Helicopter)

DESCRIPTION: The Squirrel is a small, single-engined civilian helicopter popular with TV news and radio stations. It competes with the Bell Jet Ranger so is most likely to be seen in Europe, though there are many in the US also.

POINTS VALUE: 30

(**DATE SPOTTED:**) (**SPOT IT!**) (**GOT IT!**)

(**WHERE SPOTTED:**)

(**PLANE:** Boeing V-22 Osprey)

(**CLASS:** Tilt-rotor)

DESCRIPTION: Designed to combine the best of helicopter and plane, the revolutionary Osprey takes off in helicopter mode (ie: vertically), then the giant rotor blades tilt forward and it is able to fly like a normal aircraft, before hovering again to land.

POINTS VALUE: 40

(**DATE SPOTTED:**) (**SPOT IT!**) (**GOT IT!**)

(**WHERE SPOTTED:**)

INDEX

Thanks go to the following photographers: B.Condon, Sunil Gupta, Gerhard Plomitzer, Simon Thomas, Vivian Watts, Anders Presterud, Kevin Wachter, Andreas Stocki, Thomas Posch, Neville Dawson, Jeff Claybrook, Colin Work, Ed Marmet, Dimitry Shapiro, Nik Deblauwe, United States Air Force.

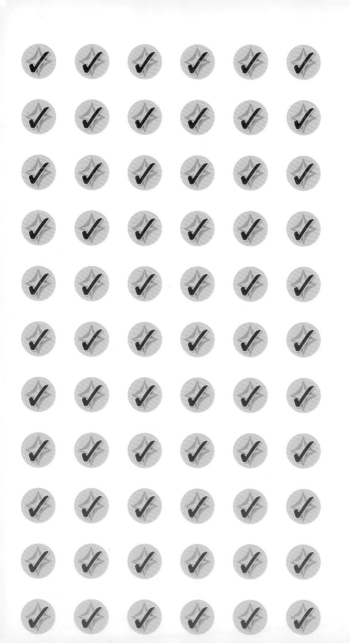

STICKER SPOT IT
AIRCRAFT

AIRCRAFT
STICKER SPOT IT

AIRCRAFT

AIRCRAFT

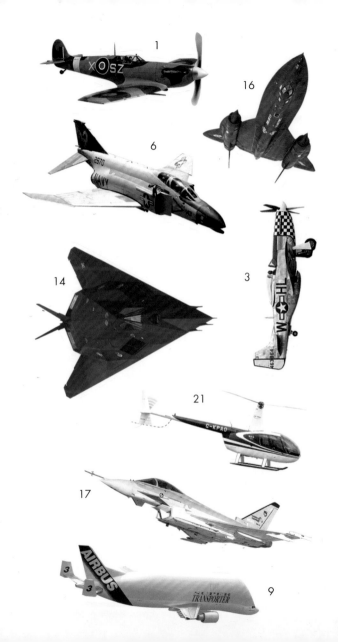